How Cars Changed the World

Kurt Hoffman

New York

Published in 2009 by The Rosen Publishing Group, Inc.
29 East 21st Street, New York, NY 10010

Book Design: Haley Wilson

Photo Credits: Cover (highways) © Glowimages/Getty Images; cover (car) © Car Culture/ Getty Images; p. 5 (wheel background) © Stephen Bonk/Shutterstock; p. 5 (man walking) © Kevin Renes/Shutterstock; p. 5 (carts and carriages) © Slobodan Djajic/Shutterstock; pp. 6–7 © Jennifer Ruch/Shutterstock; p. 9 © LouLouPhotos/Shutterstock;
p. 10 © http://en.wikipedia.org/wiki/Image:Hyundai_car_assembly_line.jpg; p. 13 © iofoto/Shutterstock.

ISBN: 978-1-4358-0119-6
6-pack ISBN: 978-1-4358-0120-2

Manufactured in the United States of America

Contents

Early Land Travel

Long ago, people walked to get from place to place. They carried, pushed, or pulled things to move them.

Then, people began to ride animals and use them to carry goods. They found that rollers made moving things easier. They put a board on top of logs, placed objects on the board, and pulled. The logs rolled and moved the board forward.

Rollers led to the invention of the wheel and **axle**. People made carts by **connecting** wheels and an axle to a board with sides.

This timeline shows the changes made over time in how people moved themselves and their things from place to place.

Early Land Travel

- man walking
- man riding horse
- roller
- cart
- horse pulling cart
- horse pulling carriage

From Carts to Carriages

Animals were used to pull carts, moving people and goods from place to place. Sides, tops, and seats were added to carts, making **carriages**.

Riding in a carriage kept people out of hot sun and bad weather.

Roads were built for the carriages. Early roads were dirt and stone. Carriage wheels were usually made of wood or iron, which made the ride bumpy. People wanted a more comfortable way to travel. They wanted a carriage that could move on its own so they wouldn't need animals to pull it.

The Car Is Invented

People built carriages that were moved by different kinds of power. These were the first cars!

Some carriages needed wind power to move. Some were powered by steam or **electric engines**. The cars were slow because it took a long time to either make the steam or power the engine.

In the late 1800s, people built cars powered by **gasoline** engines. A rubber tire filled with air was invented. Cars became faster and had a smoother ride!

Henry Ford built a car called the Model T in the early 1900s.

05

The Growth of Towns and Cities

At first, few people had enough money to buy cars. Then, Henry Ford began using a moving **assembly line** in his factory. This made it possible for workers to build cars faster and more cheaply. As a result, more people could buy cars.

Many people were needed to work on assembly lines. Workers moved to towns and cities to be near their jobs, and towns and cities grew.

In the cities, people needed to buy food and clothing. Farmers raised more crops to sell. New businesses started that made, bought, sold, and delivered goods and services.

This picture shows cars and workers on a moving assembly line.

The World Changed!

As more people drove cars, people and goods moved over greater **distances**. People began to live further away from their jobs. New communities, jobs, businesses, and services grew.

Roads were fixed and built. Gasoline stations, restaurants, and hotels were built as people traveled longer distances from home.

Today, we use cars to get to and from work or school, go shopping, or travel to new places. Cars changed the world! How do you think your life would change without cars?

This picture shows what a busy highway in a big city looks like today.

Cars Changed the World

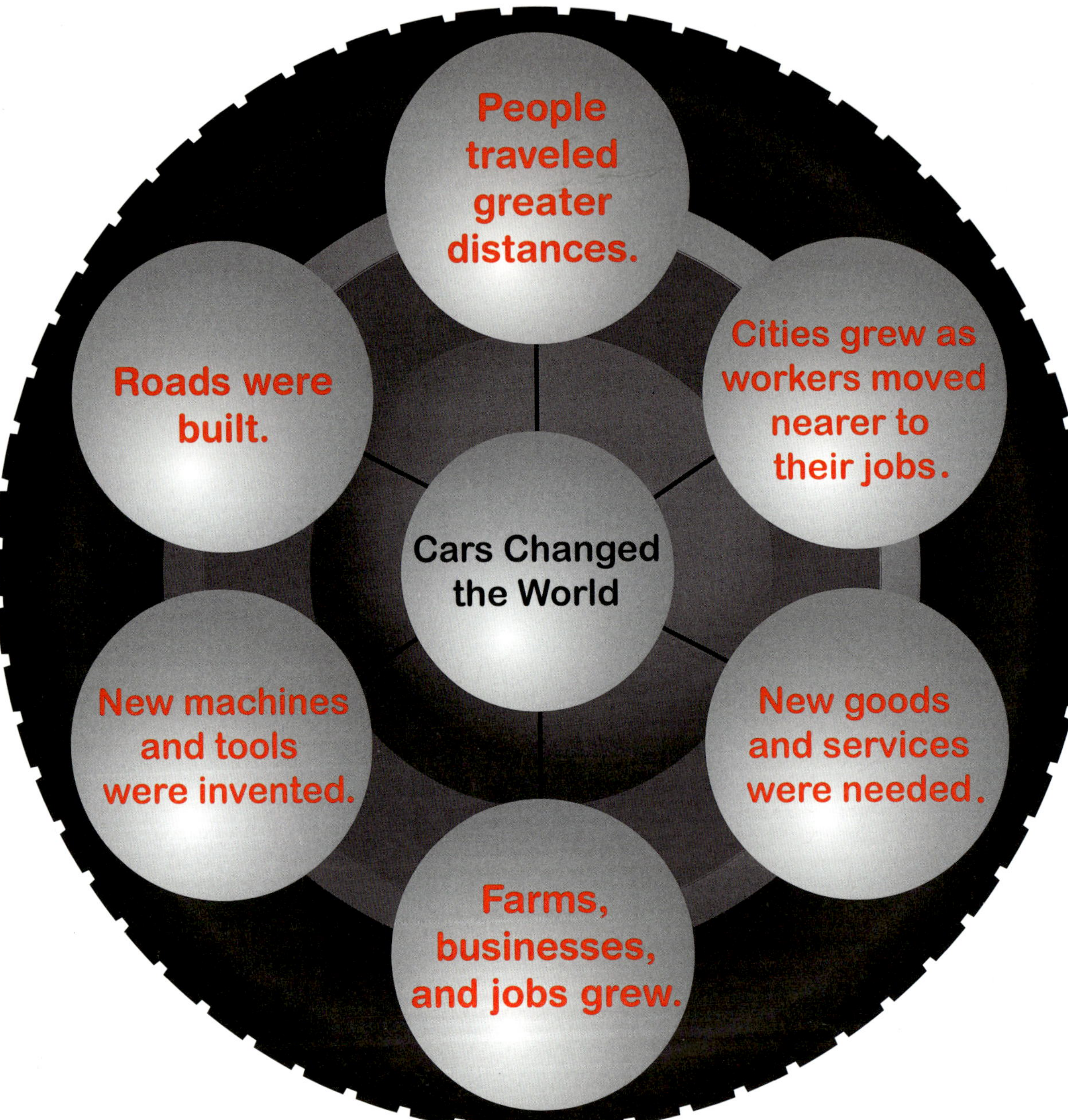

What other ways can you think of that cars changed the world?

Glossary

assembly line (uh-SEHM-blee LYN) A system for making things in which the things move down a line and each worker along the line does one job to help make the object.

axle (AK-suhl) A bar on which wheels turn.

carriage (KEHR-ihj) A wheeled object used to carry people or things.

connect (kuh-NEKT) To bind together.

distance (DIHS-tuhns) The length between two places.

electric engine (ih-LEHK-trik EHN-juhn) A machine that runs on stored energy that it turns into motion.

gasoline (GA-suh-leen) The matter that supplies energy to car engines.

Index

Due to the changing nature of Internet links, The Rosen Publishing Group, Inc., has developed an online list of Web sites related to the subject of this book. This site is updated regularly. Please use this link to access the list: http://www.rcbmlinks.com/rlr/cars